<h1 style="text-align:center">OMAN 2016 HUMAN RIGHTS REPORT</h1>

EXECUTIVE SUMMARY

The Sultanate of Oman is a hereditary monarchy ruled by Sultan Qaboos al-Said since 1970. The sultan has sole authority to enact laws through royal decree, although ministries and the bicameral Majlis Oman (parliament) can draft laws, and citizens may provide input through their elected representatives. The Majlis Oman is composed of the Majlis al-Dawla (upper house/State Council), whose 84 members are appointed by the sultan, and the elected 85-member Majlis al-Shura (lower house/Consultative Assembly). In October 2015, approximately 612,000 citizens participated in the country's Majlis al-Shura elections for the Consultative Assembly, or lower house of parliament; there were no independent observers and no notable claims of improper government interference.

The Royal Office and Royal Diwan--the sultan's personal offices--maintained control over the security forces.

The principal human rights problems were the inability of citizens to choose their government in free, fair and periodic elections based on universal and equal suffrage; limits on freedom of speech, assembly, and association; and restrictions on independent civil society.

Other concerns included lack of regular, independent inspections of prisons and detention centers; allegations of mistreatment of prisoners and detainees; insufficient protection for victims of domestic violence; sociocultural discrimination against women; and instances of expatriate foreign resident laborers subjected to labor violations, some of which amounted to forced labor. The government continued to crack down on bloggers and cyber-activists, temporarily detaining and imprisoning those who publicly criticized officials and or government policy.

Authorities generally held security personnel and other government officials accountable for their actions. The government acted against corruption during the year, with cases proceeding through the court system.

Section 1. Respect for the Integrity of the Person, Including Freedom from:

a. Arbitrary Deprivation of Life and other Unlawful or Politically Motivated Killings

There were no reports that the government or its agents committed arbitrary or unlawful killings.

b. Disappearance

There were no reports of politically motivated or forced disappearances in the country.

c. Torture and Other Cruel, Inhuman, or Degrading Treatment or Punishment

The country's law prohibits such practices; however, prisoners reported sleep deprivation, exposure to extreme temperatures, beatings, and solitary confinement.

Prison and Detention Center Conditions

Prison and detention center conditions generally met international standards.

Physical Conditions: There were no reports of overcrowding in prison and detention centers.

Administration: There was no established prison authority to which prisoners could bring grievances concerning prison conditions. There is no ombudsman to serve on behalf of prisoners and detainees; this responsibility falls under the Public Prosecutor's jurisdiction. Prisoners and detainees did not always have regular access to visitors.

The Oman Human Rights Commission (OHRC), a quasi-independent government-sanctioned body, investigated and monitored prison and detention center conditions through site visits. OHRC authorities investigated claims of abuse but did not publish the results of their investigations, purportedly to protect the privacy of the individuals involved. The OHRC published the findings of its September 27 welfare visit to the deputy supreme court justice detained by the Royal Oman Police (ROP).

Independent Monitoring: The law permitted visits by independent human rights observer groups, yet none existed in the country. There were no reports of independent, nongovernmental observers requesting to visit the country. Consular officers from certain embassies reported difficulties in meeting with prisoners.

d. Arbitrary Arrest or Detention

The law prohibits arbitrary arrest and detention, but the law permits the government to detain suspects for up to 30 days without charge.

Role of the Police and Security Apparatus

The Ministry of the Royal Office controls internal and external security and coordinates all intelligence and security policies. Under the Royal Office, the Internal Security Service (ISS) investigates all matters related to domestic security. The ROP, including the ROP Coast Guard, is also subordinate to the Royal Office and performs regular police duties, provides security at points of entry, and serves as the country's immigration and customs agency. The Ministry of Defense, particularly the Royal Army of Oman (RAO), is responsible for securing the borders and has limited domestic security responsibilities. The Sultan's Special Force (SSF) facilitates land and maritime border security in conjunction with the ROP, including rapid reaction anti-smuggling and anti-piracy capabilities. Civilian authorities maintained effective control over the ISS, the SSF, the RAO, and the ROP. There were no reports of judicial impunity involving the security forces during the year.

Arrest Procedures and Treatment of Detainees

The law does not require the ROP to obtain a warrant before making an arrest, but it stipulates that police must either release the person or refer the matter to the public prosecution within specified timeframes. For most crimes, the public prosecutor must formally arrest or release the person within 48 hours of detention; however, in cases related to security, which is broadly defined, authorities can hold individuals for up to 30 days without charge. The law requires that those arrested must be informed immediately of the charges against them. There was a functioning bail system. Detainees generally had prompt access to a lawyer of their choice. The state provided public attorneys to indigent detainees, as required by law. Authorities generally allowed detainees prompt access to family members. In cases involving foreign citizens, police sometimes failed to notify the detainee's local sponsor or the citizen's embassy.

Arbitrary Arrest: The law prohibits arbitrary arrest and detention; however, individuals can be held for up to 15 days without charge.

<u>Detainee's Ability to Challenge Lawfulness of Detention before a Court</u>: Persons arrested or detained are entitled to challenge in court the legal basis of their detention.

e. Denial of Fair Public Trial

Although the law provides for an independent judiciary, the sultan may act as a Court of Final Appeal and exercise his power of pardon as chairman of the Supreme Judicial Council, the country's highest legal body, which is empowered to review all judicial decisions. Principles of sharia (Islamic law) inform the civil, commercial, and criminal codes. The law allows women to serve as judges. Civilian or military courts try all cases.

Trial Procedures

The law provides for the right to a fair trial and stipulates the presumption of innocence. Citizens and legally resident noncitizens have the right to a public trial, except when the court decides to hold a session in private in the interest of public order or morals; the judiciary generally enforced this right. While the vast majority of legal proceedings were open to the public, authorities sometimes closed cases concerning corruption, especially cases involving senior government officials and members of the royal family. The government did not uniformly provide language interpretation for non-Arabic speakers.

Defendants have the right to consult with an attorney. Courts provide public attorneys to indigent detainees and offer legal defense for defendants facing prison terms of three years or more. The prosecution and defense counsel direct questions to witnesses through the judge. Defendants have the right to be present, submit evidence, and confront witnesses at their trials. Defendants and their lawyers generally have access to government-held evidence relevant to their cases. There is no known systemic use of forced confession or compulsion to self-incriminate during trial proceedings in the country. Those convicted in any court have one opportunity to appeal a jail sentence longer than three months and fines of more than 480 rials ($1,250) to the appellate courts. The judiciary enforced these rights for all citizens; some foreign embassies claimed these rights were not always uniformly enforced for noncitizens, particularly migrant workers.

Political Prisoners and Detainees

In an interview with Saudi newspaper *Okaz* in October and in response to a question on the number of political detainees in Oman, Minister Responsible for Foreign Affairs Yusuf bin Alawi stated that the government held a "small number," who were "activists" and "individuals."

Civil Judicial Procedures and Remedies

Civil laws govern civil cases. Citizens and foreign residents could file cases, including lawsuits seeking damages for human rights violations, but no known filings occurred during the reporting year. The Administrative Court reviews complaints about the misuse of governmental authority. It has the power to reverse decisions by government bodies and to award compensation.

Appointments to this court are subject to the approval of the Administrative Affairs Council. The court's president and deputy president are appointed by royal decree based on the council's nomination. Citizens and foreign workers may file complaints regarding working conditions with the Ministry of Manpower for alternative dispute resolution. The ministry may refer cases to the courts if it is unable to negotiate a solution.

f. Arbitrary or Unlawful Interference with Privacy, Family, Home, or Correspondence

The law does not require police to obtain search warrants before entering homes, but they usually obtain warrants from the Public Prosecutor's Office. The government monitored private communications, including cell phone, e-mail, and internet chat room exchanges. The government blocked some voice-over internet protocol sites, such as Skype and FaceTime. Authorities blocked the import of certain publications, e.g., pornography. Shipping companies claimed that customs officials sometimes confiscated these materials.

The Ministry of Interior requires citizens to obtain permission to marry foreigners, except nationals of Gulf Cooperation Council countries, whom citizens may marry without restriction; authorities do not automatically grant permission, which is particularly difficult for Omani women to obtain. Citizen marriage to a foreigner abroad without ministry approval may result in denial of entry for the foreign spouse at the border and preclude children from claiming citizenship and residency rights. It also may result in a bar from government employment and a fine of 2,000 rials ($5,200).

Despite legal protections for women from forced marriage, deeply embedded tribal practices ultimately compel most citizen women towards or away from a choice of spouse.

Section 2. Respect for Civil Liberties, Including:

a. Freedom of Speech and Press

The law provides for limited freedom of speech and press, but authorities did not always respect these rights. Journalists and writers exercised self-censorship.

Freedom of Speech and Expression: The law prohibits criticism of the sultan in any form or medium, as well as any "material that leads to public discord, violates the security of the state, or abuses a person's dignity or his rights;" "messages of any form that violate public order and morals or are harmful to a person's safety;" and "defamation of character." Therefore, it is illegal to insult any public official or private citizen, and authorities have prosecuted individuals for writing about the sultan in a way the government perceived to be negative.

In October 2015 the sultan issued a royal decree prohibiting "broadcasting or publishing any news or information or rumors targeting the prestige of the State's authorities or aimed to weaken confidence in them." This law grants the government broad powers to arrest citizens for vaguely defined infractions.

Press and Media Freedoms: Media did not operate freely. Authorities tolerated limited criticism in privately owned newspapers and magazines, although editorials generally were consistent with the government's views. Although mainstream social debate occurred in media, the government and privately owned radio and television stations did not generally broadcast political material criticizing the government. Authorities arrested bloggers during the year. On August 10, the government closed the independent newspaper *al-Zaman* and detained its managing editor, Yousef al-Hajj, chief editor, Ibrahim al-Maamari, and journalist Zaher al-Abri after they published an article on July 26 detailing corruption in the Supreme Court. The centerpiece of the allegations was an interview with the deputy chief justice, corroborating the corruption allegations. The deputy chief justice was detained and held under house arrest by the Royal Oman Police, and was visited by the Oman Human Rights Commission (OHRC). International human rights organizations and the brother of one of the *al-Zaman* employees reported that at least one of the journalists had been subjected to solitary confinement. During the trial the court refused motions by the defense attorney, to include calling witnesses and a change of judge after the judge reportedly mocked the defendants. On September 21, the presiding judge sentenced al-Hajj and al-Maamari to three years' imprisonment each. They also received 3,000 rials ($7,800) fines. The judge also sentenced al-Abri to one-year imprisonment, with a fine of 1,000 OMR ($2,600). Additionally, the judge ordered the indefinite closure of *al-Zaman*, and the journalists were released on bail.

The law criminalizes a wide variety of expression. Authorities required journalists to obtain a license to work; freelance journalists are ineligible for a license.

<u>Violence and Harassment</u>: In isolated instances authorities harassed journalists.

<u>Censorship or Content Restrictions</u>: Headlines in both public and private media print outlets were subject to an official, nontransparent review and approval process before publication. Journalists and writers exercised self-censorship. The law permits the Ministry of Information to review all media products and books produced within or imported into the country. The ministry occasionally prohibited or censored material from domestic and imported publications viewed as politically, culturally, or sexually offensive. Some books were not permitted in the country. There is only one major publishing house in the country, and publication of books remained limited. The government required religious groups to notify the Ministry of Endowments and Religious Affairs (MERA) before importing any religious materials and submit a copy for the MERA files.

<u>Libel/Slander Laws</u>: The government used libel laws and national security concerns as grounds to suppress criticism of government figures and politically objectionable views. Libel is a criminal offense, which allows for a heavy fine and prison sentence.

<u>National Security</u>: The government prohibited publication of any material that "violates the security of the state."

Internet Freedom

The law restricts free speech exercised via the internet, and the government enforces the restrictions. The government's national telecommunications company and private service providers make internet access available for a fee to citizens and foreign residents. Internet access is available via schools, workplaces, wireless networks at coffee shops, and other venues, especially in urban areas.

Authorities monitored the activities of telecommunications service providers and obliged them to block access to numerous websites considered pornographic, or culturally or politically sensitive. The criteria for blocking access to internet sites were not transparent or consistent. Authorities sometimes blocked blogs. Most video-chat technologies, such as Skype, were blocked.

The Law to Counter Information Technology Crimes allows authorities to prosecute individuals for any message sent via any medium that "violates public order and morals." The law details crimes that take place on the internet that "might prejudice public order or religious values" and specifies a penalty of between one month and a year in prison and fines of not less than 1,000 rials ($2,600). Authorities also applied the law against bloggers and social media users who insult the sultan.

The government placed warnings on websites informing users that criticism of the sultan or personal criticism of government officials would be censored and could lead to police questioning, effectively increasing self-censorship.

Website administrators or moderators were cautious concerning content and were reportedly quick to delete potentially offensive material in chat rooms, on social networking fora, and on blog postings. Some website administrators posted warnings exhorting users to follow local laws and regulations.

Academic Freedom and Cultural Events

The government restricted academic freedom and cultural events. Academics largely practiced self-censorship. Colleges and universities were required to have permission from the Ministry of Foreign Affairs and the Ministry of Higher Education before meeting with foreign diplomatic missions or accepting money for programs or speakers.

The government censored publicly shown films, primarily for sexual content and nudity. The government restricted the ability of bands with three or more members to perform in public venues. Dancing in restaurants and entertainment venues without a permit also was forbidden by law.

In August the government closed the AMIDEAST Muscat office, which had prepared local students for education abroad. The office had also facilitated cultural exchange.

b. Freedom of Peaceful Assembly and Association

Freedom of Assembly

The law provides for limited freedom of assembly, but the government restricted this right. Government approval was necessary for all public gatherings of more than nine persons, although there was no clear process for obtaining approval for public demonstrations. Authorities enforced this requirement sporadically. A 2014 report from the UN special rapporteur on rights to freedom of peaceful assembly expressed concern with government attempts to limit assembly and association rights and stated that individuals seeking reform were "afraid to speak their minds, afraid to speak on the telephone, afraid to meet."

Private-sector employees in the energy and industrial manufacturing sectors threatened strikes in isolated cases. In all cases workers threatened to picket to protest company downsizing. These did not occur, however, because company leadership used incentives, like promises of job security and other material benefits, to persuade organizers to call off the strike. The threat alone of a strike or demonstration was sufficient to compel management to negotiate with the workers, resolving the underlying issue (see section 7.a.).

Freedom of Association

The law provides for freedom of association for undefined "legitimate objectives and in a proper manner." Examples of such associations include labor unions and social groups for foreign nationalities, such as the Indian Social Group. The Council of Ministers limited freedom of association in practice by prohibiting associations whose activities it deemed "inimical to the social order" or otherwise not appropriate. A royal decree in 2014 promulgated a new nationality law that stipulates citizens joining groups deemed harmful to national interests could be subject to revocation of citizenship.

Associations must register with the Ministry of Social Development, which approves all associations' bylaws and determines whether a group serves the interest of the country. The average time required to register an association ranged from two months to two years. Approval time varied based on the level of preparedness of the applying organization and the subject matter of the organization, as well its leadership and focus of the organization's mission. The approval time was often longer when a group required significant help from the ministry to formalize its structure. Formal registration of nationality-based associations was limited to one association for each nationality. For example, the Indian Social Group had many different subcommittees based on language and geography.

Associations are forbidden from receiving funding from international groups or foreign governments without government approval. Individuals convicted of accepting foreign funding for an association may receive up to six months in jail and a fine of 500 rials ($1,300). Foreign diplomatic missions are required to request meetings with nongovernmental organizations (NGOs) through the Ministry of Foreign Affairs by diplomatic note. NGOs may not meet with foreign diplomatic missions and foreign organizations without prior approval from the Ministry of Foreign Affairs. The government robustly enforced this law, stopping most foreign funding of educational and public diplomacy programs pending a government-wide review.

c. Freedom of Religion

See the Department of *State's International Religious Freedom Report* at www.state.gov/religiousfreedomreport/.

d. Freedom of Movement, Internally Displaced Persons, Protection of Refugees, and Stateless Persons

The law provides for freedom of movement within the country and repatriation and the government generally respected these rights. Citizens could generally travel freely outside the country, although that right is not codified. The Office of the UN High Commissioner for Refugees (UNHCR) occasionally visited the country but did not maintain an office or personnel in the country.

Abuse of Migrants, Refugees, and Stateless Persons: During the year Human Rights Watch (HRW) released a report, based primarily on interviews with 59 female domestic workers, claiming widespread abuse and exploitation of migrant domestic works in the country. The country has a large number of female migrant workers from India, Nepal, Bangladesh, Sri Lanka, Ethiopia, Indonesia, and the Philippines, and in the report many of these workers described abuses that amounted to forced labor or trafficking. According to HRW, "female migrant domestic workers faced multiple forms of discrimination and arbitrary government policies: as domestic workers, they are excluded from equal labor law protections guaranteed to other workers; as women, regulations provide that they can be paid less than male domestic workers; and as migrants, their salaries are based on their national origin rather than their skills and experience."

According to the report, the country criminalizes slavery and trafficking, but enforcement is weak. Although forced labor is punished under the country's labor law, domestic workers are excluded from that law's protections. Authorities prosecuted a few individuals for forced labor, but it was unclear whether any of those cases involved domestic workers.

There was a high number of reports of women trafficked into forced labor from the neighboring UAE, but there were only five sex trafficking prosecutions in 2015, and none reported on forced labor. Approximately one-quarter of the domestic workers HRW interviewed said that their employers physically or sexually abused them by shouting, threatening to kill them, or calling them insulting names.

In-country Movement: There are no official government restrictions on internal travel for any citizen. The government must approve official travel by foreign diplomats to the Dhofar and Musandam regions. There were reports of many migrant domestic workers having their passports confiscated by employers, who sponsor the foreign workers.

Employers have an inordinate amount of control over these workers, according to HRW. Migrant workers cannot work for a new employer without the permission of their current employer, even if they complete their contract and the current employer is abusive. Employers can have a worker's visa canceled arbitrarily. Workers who leave their jobs without the consent of their employer can be punished with fines, deportation, reentry bans, or forcible return to the abusive employer.

Foreign Travel: Some foreigners must obtain an exit visa from their employer prior to leaving the country. Exit visas may be denied when there is a dispute over payment or work remaining, leaving the foreign citizen in country with recourse only through local courts. Courts provided recourse to workers denied exit visas, but the process was opaque. In a few cases, travel bans--through confiscation of passports--were imposed on citizens involved in political activism.

Protection of Refugees

Access to Asylum: The laws provide for the granting of asylum or refuge for internally displaced persons, and the government has established a system for providing protection. The ROP reportedly granted asylum and accepted displaced persons for resettlement during the year. The ROP's system for granting asylum and resettlement is not transparent, and the law does not specify a timeframe in which the ROP must adjudicate an asylum application.

Refoulement: The government generally did not provide protection to refugees from repatriation to countries where their lives or freedom would be threatened. Tight control over the entry of foreigners effectively limited access to protection for refugees and asylum seekers. Authorities apprehended and deported hundreds of presumed economic migrants from Somalia, Ethiopia, and Eritrea who sought to enter the country illegally by land and sea from the south. Afghans and Pakistanis generally came to the country by boat via Iran. Authorities generally detained these persons in centers in Salalah or the northern port city of Sohar, where they were held an average of one month before deportation to their countries of origin.

Access to Basic Services: Without an official sponsor, it was difficult for economic migrants to have access to basic services, such as health care. Many applied to their embassies for repatriation. Some asylum seekers developed strong relationships within their community that informally provided for them while they sought new employment.

Section 3. Freedom to Participate in the Political Process

The law does not provide citizens the ability to choose their government in free and fair periodic elections based on universal and equal suffrage. The sultan retains ultimate authority on all foreign and domestic issues. With the exception of the military and other security forces, all citizens who have reached 21 years of age have the right to vote for candidates for the Consultative Council and the provincial councils.

Elections and Political Participation

Recent Elections: In October 2015, approximately 612,000 citizens participated in the country's Majlis al-Shura elections for the consultative assembly, or lower house of parliament. Electoral commissions reviewed potential candidates against a set of objective educational and character criteria (at least a high school education and no criminal history or mental illness) before they allowed candidates' names on the ballot. The Ministry of Interior administered and closely monitored campaign materials and events. There were no notable or widespread allegations of fraud or improper government interference in the voting process. The government did not allow independent monitoring of the elections.

Political Parties and Political Participation: The law does not allow political parties, and citizens did not attempt to form them.

Participation of Women and Minorities: During the Majlis al-Shura elections in October 2015, voters elected one woman as a representative. The sultan appointed 13 women to the 84-member State Council and three women to the 29-member Council of Ministers. Government policy does not recognize minority groups, who participated in political life and have roles in government. There were no self-identified minority communities.

Section 4. Corruption and Lack of Transparency in Government

Corruption: The law provides criminal penalties for official corruption, and the government generally implemented these laws effectively. In previous years there were reports of government corruption, including in police, ministries, and state-owned companies.

Financial Disclosure: Public officials are subject to financial disclosure laws. When selected for disclosure, officials are required to list their finances, business interests, and property, as well as that of their spouses and children. These records are made public, and there are fines associated with noncompliance. The State Audit Authority monitors this process.

Public Access to Information: The law does not provide for public access to government information, although the government published all royal decrees and ministerial decisions in the *Official Gazette*.

Section 5. Governmental Attitude Regarding International and Nongovernmental Investigation of Alleged Violations of Human Rights

No autonomous, officially sanctioned, domestic human rights organizations existed. There were civil society groups that advocated for persons protected under human rights conventions, particularly women and persons with disabilities. These groups were required to register with the Ministry of Social Development.

The government did not support international or domestic human rights organizations operating in the country.

Government Human Rights Bodies: The NHRC, a government-funded commission made up of members from the public, private, and academic sectors, reported on human rights to the sultan via the State Council. The NHRC also conducted prison visits and continued a community and school outreach program to discuss human rights with students.

Section 6. Discrimination, Societal Abuses, and Trafficking in Persons

Women

Rape and Domestic Violence: The law criminalizes rape with penalties of up to 15 years in prison but does not criminalize spousal rape. The government generally enforced the law when individuals reported cases, but there were indications that many victims did not report rape because of cultural and societal factors. In previous years police charged individuals with rape or attempted rape. Foreign nationals working as domestic employees occasionally reported that their sponsors or employees of labor recruitment agencies had sexually abused them. According to diplomatic observers, police investigations resulted in few rape convictions.

The law does not specifically address domestic violence, and judicial protection orders from domestic violence do not exist. Charges could be brought, however, under existing statutes outlawing assault, battery, and aggravated assault, which can carry a maximum sentence of three years in prison. Allegations of spousal abuse in civil courts handling family law cases reportedly were common. Victims of domestic violence may file a complaint with police, and reports suggested that police responded promptly and professionally.

Female Genital Mutilation/Cutting (FGM/C): The law prohibits female genital mutilation/cutting (FGM/C) in hospitals and clinics but does not explicitly ban the practice. There were no reliable statistics on the prevalence of FGM/C, but some reports suggested it was practiced. According to press reports, a 2010 Ministry of Health study on FGM/C found that men and women across all ages broadly accepted the practice, especially in rural areas. In the southern Dhofar region, FGM/C reportedly was performed on newborns and involved a partial or total clitoridectomy (Type I as defined by the World Health Organization). Throughout the rest of the country, Type IV is reportedly most prevalent. According to local sources, an older female relative with no medical training typically performed the practice in unhygienic conditions.

Officials at the National Human Rights Commission and Ministry of Social Development claimed that language in the 2014 Child Law prohibits FGM/C as a harmful traditional practice, although the law does not explicitly describe types of FGM/C practices. As of the end of 2015, there was no public outreach to educate citizens about the provisions of the new law or about the harmful effects of FGM/C.

Sexual Harassment: The country does not have a law against sexual harassment. Sexual harassment has been effectively prosecuted using statutes prohibiting offensive language and behavior. Nonetheless, a 2010 Freedom House report on women's rights in the Middle East indicated that female employees were discouraged from reporting sexual harassment for fear of losing their jobs and because social pressure places responsibility on them for "proper moral behavior."

Reproductive Rights: The government recognized the right of married couples to decide the number, spacing, and timing of their children; to manage their reproductive health; and to have access to the information and means to do so, free from discrimination, coercion, or violence. Health clinics freely disseminated information on family planning under the guidance of the Ministry of Health. Some forms of birth control, including condoms, were available at pharmacies and supermarkets, although doctor-prescribed birth control medication was generally not available for unmarried women. According to 2016 UN Population Fund estimates, only 25 percent of women aged 15-49 were using a modern method of contraceptives, and 28 percent of women had an unmet need for family planning. The government provided free childbirth services to citizens within the framework of universal health care. Prenatal and postnatal care was readily available and used. Men and women received equal access to diagnosis and treatment for sexually transmitted infections, including HIV/AIDS; however, social taboos prevented individuals from seeking treatment.

Discrimination: The law prohibits gender-based discrimination against citizens. Local interpretations of Islamic law and practice of cultural traditions, in social and legal institutions discriminated against women. In some personal status cases, such as divorce, a woman's testimony is equal to half that of a man. The legal provision that allows men to divorce their wives with the signature of two witnesses is not accorded to women. The law favors male heirs in adjudicating inheritance. Women married to noncitizens may not transmit citizenship to their children and cannot sponsor their noncitizen husband's presence in the country. Men can marry up to four wives and do not require consent from existing wives to marry additional wives.

The law provides for transmission of citizenship at birth if the father is a citizen; if the mother is a citizen and the father is unknown; or if a child of unknown parents is found in the country. The law provides that an adult may become a citizen by applying for citizenship and subsequently residing legally in the country for 20 years or 10 years if married to a male citizen. During that time an applicant cannot reside more than one month of each year outside the country. A person seeking naturalization is expected first to give up any previous citizenship.

Women cannot transmit citizenship to their spouses or children. Observers reported a few isolated cases of children without documentation as the result of a marriage between an Omani woman and a non-Omani man. These children are not eligible for citizenship and are vulnerable to being stateless. Under the law, women--regardless of marital status--have equal property ownership rights as men. The law equalizes the treatment of men and women in receiving free government land for housing.

Government policy provided women with equal opportunities for education, and this policy effectively eliminated the previous gender gap in educational attainment. Although some educated women held positions of authority in government, business, and media, many women faced job discrimination based on cultural norms. The law entitles women to paid maternity leave and equal pay for equal work. The government, the largest employer of women, observed such regulations, as did many private-sector employers. Economic studies conducted by the World Economic Forum from 2015, however, showed that women earned 68 percent less than men and that their unemployment rate was at least twice as high. According to the forum, only 31 percent of women participated in the work force.

The local business community reported that the Ministry of Manpower increasingly rejected work permits for foreign women regardless of profession or country of origin, while it granted work permits to foreign men applying for comparable positions. Ministry officials said the purpose of the ban on female foreign visas was to "regularize" the labor market, without further explanation.

The Ministry of Social Development is the umbrella Ministry for Women's Affairs. The ministry provided support for women's economic development through the Oman Women's Associations and local community development centers. The government has a committee to monitor the country's compliance with the UN Convention on the Elimination of All Forms of Discrimination against Women.

Children

Birth Registration: Citizenship is derived from the father. Women married to noncitizens may not transmit citizenship to their children, and there were a few reported cases of stateless children based on this law. Children of unknown parents are automatically eligible for citizenship. Government employees raised abandoned children in an orphanage. Such children receive free education through the university level and a job following graduation. Citizen marriage to a foreigner abroad without ministry approval may preclude children from claiming citizenship rights (see section 1.f.).

Education: Primary school education for citizen children was free and universal up to age 16. The law mandates children attend school through age 10.

Child Abuse: The Ministry of Health reported a small number of cases of child abuse approximately twenty cases per year. The ministry noted that sexual abuse most commonly involved children of both sexes between the ages of six to 12 and was committed by close relatives or friends of the family. There was a heavy social stigma against reporting child abuse. According to the Child Law, any concerned citizen may report child abuse, and each governorate had an interagency committee that would meet to discuss the allegations and possibly take the child out of the parent's custody until the allegations was investigated.

Early and Forced Marriage: The age of legal marriage for men and women is 18 years, although a judge may permit a person to marry younger when the judge or family deemed the marriage was in the minor's interest. Child marriage occurred in rural communities as a traditional practice.

Female Genital Mutilation/Cutting: See information for girls under 18 in women's section above.

Sexual Exploitation of Children: Commercial sexual exploitation of children and child pornography are punishable by no fewer than five years' imprisonment. All sex outside of marriage is illegal, but sex with a minor under age 15 carries a heavier penalty (up to 15 years' imprisonment). Authorities do not charge minors. The country is not a destination for child sex tourism, and child prostitution was rare. Soliciting a child for prostitution is prohibited.

<u>International Child Abductions</u>: The country is not a party to the 1980 Hague Convention on the Civil Aspects of International Child Abduction. See the Department of State's *Annual Report on International Parental Child Abduction* at travel.state.gov/content/childabduction/en/legal/compliance.html.

Anti-Semitism

There was no indigenous Jewish population. There were no reports of anti-Semitic acts, incidents against foreign resident Jews, or public statements by community leaders or officials.

Trafficking in Persons

See the Department of State's *Trafficking in Persons Report* at www.state.gov/j/tip/rls/tiprpt/.

Persons with Disabilities

The law provides persons with disabilities, including physical, sensory, intellectual, and mental disabilities, the same rights as other citizens in employment, education, access to health care, and the provision of other state services. Persons with disabilities, however, continued to face discrimination. The law mandates access to buildings for persons with disabilities, but many older buildings, including government buildings and schools, did not to conform to the law. The law also requires private enterprises employing more than 50 persons to reserve at least 2 percent of positions for persons with disabilities. Authorities did not systematically enforce this regulation.

No protective legislation provides for equal educational opportunities for persons with disabilities. The government provided alternative education opportunities for more than 500 children with disabilities, including overseas schooling when appropriate; this was largely due to lack of capacity within the country.

Additionally, the Ministry of Education collaborated with the International Council for Educational Reform and Development to create a curriculum for students with mental disabilities within the standard school system, which was in place throughout the year. There were a number of civil society groups raising awareness of the experiences and needs of persons with disabilities.

The Ministry of Social Development is responsible for protecting the rights of persons with disabilities. The Directorate General of Disabled Affairs within the Ministry of Social Development creates programs for persons with disabilities, and implements these programs in coordination with relevant authorities. The directorate was authorized further to supervise all of the ministry's rehabilitation and treatment centers for persons with disabilities.

Acts of Violence, Discrimination, and Other Abuses Based on Sexual Orientation and Gender Identity

Lesbian, gay, bisexual, transgender, and intersex (LGBTI) persons faced legal, institutional, and social discrimination. The penal code criminalizes consensual same-sex sexual conduct with a jail term of six months to three years. Social and cultural norms reinforced discrimination against openly LGBTI persons.

Public discussion of sexual orientation and gender identity remained a social taboo, and authorities took steps to block LGBTI-related internet content. Observers believed that social stigma and intimidation prevented LGBTI persons from reporting incidents of violence or abuse.

Transgender persons were not recognized as a gender class by the government and were not afforded protection from discrimination.

There are no known LGBTI organizations active in the country; however, there are regional human rights organizations that focused on the human rights of LGBTI Omanis. There were no pride marches or LGBTI rights advocacy events.

Information was not available on official or private discrimination in employment, occupation, housing, statelessness, or access to education or health care based on sexual orientation and gender identity. There were no government efforts to address potential discrimination.

HIV and AIDS Social Stigma

Foreigners seeking residency in the country are tested for HIV/AIDS. An HIV test is performed as part of the residency application. If tested positive, the residency permission is denied, and foreigners must leave the country, but there were no known occurrences of this.

Section 7. Worker Rights

a. Freedom of Association and the Right to Collective Bargaining

The law provides that workers can form and join unions, as well as conduct legal strikes and bargain collectively, but with significant restrictions. The law provides for one general federation, to which all unions must affiliate, and which represents unions in regional and international fora. The law requires an absolute majority of an enterprise's employees to approve a strike, and notice must be given to employers three weeks in advance of the intended strike date. The law allows for collective bargaining; regulations require employers to engage in collective bargaining on the terms and conditions of employment, including wages and hours of work. Where there is no trade union, collective bargaining may take place between the employer and five representatives selected by workers. The employer may not reject any of the representatives selected. While negotiation is underway, the employer may not act on decisions related to problems under discussion. The law prohibits employers from firing or imposing penalties on employees for union activity, although it does not require reinstatement for workers fired for union activity.

Despite the legal protections in place for labor unions, no independent organized labor unions existed. Worker rights continued to be administered and directed by the General Federation of Oman Trade Unions.

Government-approved unions are open to all legal workers regardless of nationality. The law prohibits members of the armed forces, other public-security institutions, government employees, and domestic workers from forming or joining such unions.

The law prohibits unions from accepting grants or financial assistance from any source without the ministry's prior approval. By law unions must notify the government at least one month in advance of union meetings.

The government generally enforced applicable laws effectively and respected the right to collectively bargain and conduct strikes, though strikes in the oil and gas industries are forbidden. In 2015 the government did not enforce the requirements for advance notice of strikes and union meetings. The government provided an alternative dispute resolution mechanism through the Ministry of Manpower, which acted as mediator between the employer and employee for minor disputes such as disagreement over wages. If not resolved to the employee's satisfaction, the employee could, and often did, resort to the courts for relief. The country lacked dedicated labor courts, and observers noted the mandatory grievance procedures were confusing to many workers, especially foreign workers. The Ministry of Manpower had sufficient resources to act in dispute resolution, and there were no complaints of lengthy delays or appeals.

Freedom of association in union matters and the right to collective bargaining exist, but often the threat of a strike can prompt either company action to resolution, or spur government intervention. Strikes rarely occurred and were generally resolved quickly, sometimes through government mediation.

b. Prohibition of Forced or Compulsory Labor

The law prohibits all forced or compulsory labor, but domestic workers are not covered by the law. All police officials underwent training in how to identify victims of trafficking in persons to help them identify cases of forced or compulsory labor. There were no reports of police taking actions directly to eliminate forced labor; their focus was on identifying and arresting foreign workers without proper work authorization. Police officials reportedly raided a shelter for abused domestic workers operated by a foreign embassy and deported all the workers without any investigation for trafficking in persons.

Conditions indicative of forced labor were present. By law all foreign workers, who comprised approximately one-half of the workforce and the majority of workers in some sectors, must be sponsored by a citizen employer or accredited diplomatic mission. Some men and women from South and Southeast Asia, employed as domestic workers or low-skilled workers in the construction, agriculture, and service sectors, faced working conditions indicative of forced labor, including withholding of passports, restrictions on movement, usurious recruitment fees, nonpayment of wages, long working hours without food or rest, threats, and physical or sexual abuse. Authorities continued to rely on victims to identify themselves and report abuses voluntarily, rather than proactively investigating trafficking in vulnerable communities.

Sponsorship requirements left workers vulnerable to exploitative conditions, as it was difficult for an employee to change sponsors (see section 2.d.). The "free visa" system, in which sponsors allow employees to work for other employers in return for a fee, leaves workers vulnerable to exploitation. Some employers of domestic workers, contrary to law, withheld passports and other documents, complicating workers' release from unfavorable contracts and preventing workers' departure after their work contracts expired. In some cases employers demanded exorbitant release fees totaling as much as 700 rials ($1,820) before providing a "release letter" to permit the worker to change employers. Without this release letter, foreign workers were required to either depart the country for a minimum of two years, or remain in their current position. There were reports that sponsors were reluctant to provide release letters, which would result in loss of the foreign labor certificate for that position.

Also see the Department of State's *Trafficking in Persons Report* at www.state.gov/j/tip/rls/tiprpt/.

c. Prohibition of Child Labor and Minimum Age for Employment

The minimum age for employment is 16 years, or 18 for certain hazardous occupations; however, the government has delayed the publication of a list of prohibited hazardous occupations for several years. Children between the ages of 16 and 18 may work only between the hours of 6 a.m. and 6 p.m. and are prohibited from working for more than six hours per day, on weekends, or on holidays. The law allows exceptions to the age requirement in agricultural works, fishing, industrial works, handicrafts, and administration jobs, under the conditions that it is a one-family business and does not hinder the juvenile's education or affect health or growth.

The Ministry of Manpower and ROP are responsible for enforcing laws with respect to child labor and had sufficient resources to do so. The law provides for fines for minor violations and imprisonment for repeat violations. Employers are given time to correct practices that may be deemed child labor.

In 2015 the government made a moderate advancement in efforts to eliminate the worst forms of child labor by publishing information on child labor and drafting regulations outlining the conditions in which children may engage in light work. The government also established a Child Protection Committee to receive complaints related to violations of children's rights, including the worst forms of child labor. Although the problem did not appear to be widespread, limited reports noted that some children were engaged in child labor, especially in the agricultural sector.

Also see the Department of Labor's *Findings on the Worst Forms of Child Labor* at www.dol.gov/ilab/reports/child-labor/findings/.

d. Discrimination with Respect to Employment and Occupation

Labor laws and regulations do not address discrimination based on race, sex, gender, nationality, political views, disability, language, sexual orientation, and/or gender identity, HIV-positive status or other communicable diseases, or social status. Discrimination occurred based on sex, gender, sexual orientation, and gender identity. For further discussion of discrimination, see section 6.

e. Acceptable Conditions of Work

The minimum wage for citizens was 325 rials ($845) per month. Minimum wage regulations do not apply to a variety of occupations and businesses, including small businesses employing fewer than five persons, dependent family members working for a family firm, or some categories of manual laborers. The minimum wage does not apply to noncitizens in any occupation. Most of the citizens who lived in poverty, about 8 percent, were engaged in traditional subsistence agriculture, herding, or fishing, and generally did not benefit from the minimum wage. The private-sector workweek is 45 hours and includes a two-day rest period following five consecutive days of work. Government workers have a 35-hour workweek. The law mandates overtime pay for hours in excess of 45 per week.

The government sets occupational health and safety standards. The law states an employee may leave dangerous work conditions without jeopardy to continued employment if the employer was aware of the danger and did not implement corrective measures. Employees covered under the labor law may receive compensation for job-related injury or illness through employer-provided medical insurance.

Neither wage and hour nor occupational safety and health regulations apply to domestic workers.

The Ministry of Manpower is responsible for enforcing labor laws, and it employed approximately 90 inspectors in Muscat and an additional 70 around the country in 2015. It generally enforced the law effectively with respect to citizens; however, it did not effectively enforce regulations regarding hours of employment and working conditions for foreign workers.

Labor inspectors with arrest authority for egregious violations performed random checks of worksites to verify compliance with all labor laws. Approximately 180 inspectors from the Department of Health and Safety of the Labor Care Directorate are responsible for enforcement of health and safety codes, although limited inspections of private-sector worksites are required by law to deter or redress unsafe working conditions in the most dangerous sectors.

The ministry effectively enforced the minimum wage for citizens. No minimum wage existed for noncitizens. In wage cases the Ministry of Manpower processed complaints and acted as mediator. In a majority of cases, the plaintiff prevailed, gaining compensation, the opportunity to seek alternative employment, or return to their country of origin in the case of foreign laborers, although they rarely used the courts to seek redress. The ministry was generally effective in cases regarding minor labor disputes; however, it did not refer any egregious violations to the courts during the year.

The government made insufficient efforts during the year to prevent violations or improve wages and working conditions, which disproportionately affected foreign workers.

Foreign workers were vulnerable to poor, dangerous, or exploitative working conditions. There were reports that migrant laborers in some firms and households who worked more than 12 hours a day without a day off for below-market wages. Employers often cancelled the employment contracts of seriously sick or injured foreign workers, forcing them to return to their countries of origin or remain in the country illegally. Frequently, labor inspections focused on enforcing visa violations and deporting those in an irregular work visa status rather than verifying safe and adequate work conditions. Some foreign diplomats reported that sponsors of foreign workers were required to pay health, life, and accident insurance for female, but not male, workers and suggested that men were predominantly working in more dangerous sectors, such as construction and agriculture, which posed a higher risk of injury.

There are no maximum work-hour limits for domestic workers nor any mandatory rest periods, although the contract between the employer and worker can specify such requirements. There were frequent reports that domestic workers were subject to overwork with inadequate rest periods. Separate domestic employment regulations obligate the employer to provide domestic workers with free local medical treatment throughout the contract period. Penalties for noncompliance with health regulations were insufficient to deter violations, ranging from approximately 10 to 100 rials ($26 to $260), multiplying per occurrence per worker and doubled upon recurrence. Some domestic workers were subjected to abusive conditions.

There was little data available on workplace fatalities or safety.